The Vibrant Violin

Music Theory Book 1

A theory book especially for violin players
covering Grades 1-2

All the basics to get you going.

Easy to follow explanations,

puzzles and more.

All with the beginner violin player in mind.

Amanda Oosthuizen

Jemima Oosthuizen

The Vibrant Violin Series

Wild Music Publications

www.wildmusicpublications.com

We hope you enjoy *The Vibrant Violin Music Theory Book 1.*

Take a look at our other exciting books, including: 50+ Greatest Classics, Catch the Beat, Christmas Duets, Easy Tunes from Around the World, Trick or Treat – A Halloween Suite, Champagne and Chocolate, Fish 'n' Ships, and many more solo and duet books.

For more info on other amazing books, please go to:

WildMusicPublications.com

Visit our secret page for a **free backing track,** and more fun things for free! visit:

http://WildMusicPublications.com/**725secret-violin-track942k/**

And use the password: **m@dStrings4U!**

Happy Music Making!

The Wild Music Publications Team

To keep up –to-date with our new releases, why not **follow us on Twitter**

@WMPublications

To play the Violin well, you need to read music and understand the mysteries of music theory. The Vibrant Violin Music Theory Book 1 includes all the basics you'll need up to Grade 2 Violin and is written with the beginner Violin player in mind. Take it slowly, complete a little bit at a time and have fun!

Each section explains a new aspect of music in an easy-to-read way and is followed by exercises and puzzles to help you remember what you've learnt.

 Writing activities are shown by a Violin pencil.

After several sections, you will find a Check page where you can see how much you have remembered and keep score.

At the end of the book, there are Violin information pages, more puzzles, a list of musical terms and symbols and a chart where you can keep a record of the sections you have completed.

If you want to check your **ANSWERS**, a free answer book download is available on the **SECRET VIOLIN PAGE** of our website. Find out how to get there on the second page of the book.

When you have finished, take a look at Book 2. It includes all the crazy theory you need to know from Grades 3 – 5 Violin including: ornaments, more Violin facts, making scales, compound time signatures and much more.

Contents

Treble Clef

Violin music is written in treble clef.

Treble clef is also called G clef.

Music is written on five lines called a staff (or stave).

The treble clef is drawn at the start of every staff.

 Staff

Music is divided into measures by bar lines.

 Draw a treble clef in every measure. It may help to start by curling around a dot on the second line.

The end of a section of music is shown by a double bar line.

The end of a piece of music is shown by a final bar line.

Phrase A phrase is a short section of music that makes sense, rather like a sentence.

Phrases are shown by a large slur.

Phrases are often four measures long.

Letter Names

Notes are written on the lines and in the spaces.

The lower sounds are at the bottom of the staff.

E F G A B C D E F

Notes in the spaces spell FACE

F A C E

Write the letter names under these notes.

F

example

Write these notes in the spaces.

F A C E

Notes on the lines

E G B D F

Every Green Bus Drives Fast

Write the letter names under these notes.

E

example

Write your own selection of notes on the lines.

4

Write the letter names under these notes in the spaces.

F
....
example

Write the letter names under these notes on the lines.

G
....
example

Write your own selection of notes on lines and in spaces.

Write the letter names under these notes on lines and in spaces.

....

....

....

....

Write the notes in spaces above the letter names.

example

F   C   A   E   F   C   A   F   E   C

Write the notes on lines above the letter names.

example

B   G   E   F   D   E   G   B   D   F

Write the notes on lines or spaces above the letter names.

example

F   G   A   B   B   C   D   E   E   D   C   B

example

A   G   F   E   G   B   D   F   E   C   A   F

Write notes in lines and spaces starting from the bottom of the staff.

Write the letter names beneath the notes.

B
example   ....

....

C
example   ....

....

6

Write these words in music.

example

A   C   E   D   A   D

D   A   B   B   E   D   F   A   C   E

B   A   B   E   D   E   F   A   C   E   D

B   E   A   D   E   D   F   E   E   D   B   A   G

Write the letter names under the notes.

E
example ....

....

....

Write a phrase of music beginning and ending on C.

Note Values

Whole note - 4 counts

Write a whole note in every measure.

Dotted half note - 3 counts

Write a dotted half note in every measure.

Half note - 2 counts

Write a half note in every measure.

Qaurter note - 1 count

Write a quarter note in every measure.

Write a mixed selection of note values on the notes A and B.

8 Write the number of counts.

2
example

Ties

A tie is a loop joining notes that are the same. It means add the notes together.

♩ ♩. = 2 + 3

Write the counts and do the sum.

2 + 1 = 3
....
example

.... + ... = ...

.... + ... = ...

.... + + ... = ...

.... + + ... = ...

.... + ... = ====

.... + ... = ====

Write in the missing notes below the *.

*   *   *

3 counts   9 counts   5 counts

Write notes that make each measure add up to four quarter notes.

Write notes that make each measure add up to three quarter notes.

Using G, A, B and C, (all on the staff) write notes of different lengths.

 Match the boxes with the correct number of counts.

 Copy this music exactly.

Stems

The stems are on the left when they go down.

All notes except whole notes have stems.

The stems are on the right when they go up.

The stem goes down if a note is above the middle line.

The stem goes up if a note is below the middle line.

The stem of D on the middle line can go either up or down.

 Add a stem to each of these noteheads.

 Write a mixture of low and high noteheads and then add the stems.

Rests

Rests show silence instead of notes.

Whoile note rest

Also a full measure's rest

Half note rest

Quarter note rest

2
2 measures rest

164
164 measures rest

Dotted Minim rest

Match the boxes with the correct number of counts.

4

3

2

1

Draw the rest to match the note.

*   *   *

Draw in the rests that make every measure add up to four beats.

*   *   *   *   *   *

Fill every measure with notes and rests so that they add up to four, and then play it!

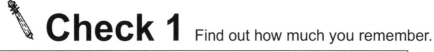 **Check 1** Find out how much you remember.

Well done! You have already completed five sections.

Mix and Match
Match the symbol to its name and number of beats.

Four quarter notes ♩ Quarter rest

One quarter rest ♩ Half note

Two quarter notes 𝅝 Quarter note

One quarter note 𝄽 Whole note

Quick Check
Are the letters correct. Tick or cross the answers.

G B C E   G A F E   D A B G   C F A A

Quiz
True or false? Circle the right answer.

1. Music is divided into measures by bar lines. True False

2. Music is written on four lines called a staff. True False

3. Music uses the first eight letters of the alphabet. True False

4. Violin music is written mostly in bass clef. True False

5. A whole note is worth two half noites. True False

6. In music silence is shown by rests. True False

How many did you get right?

Time Signatures

$\frac{2}{4}$ 2 quarter note beats in a measure

$\frac{3}{4}$ 3 quarter note beats in a measure

$\frac{4}{4}$ or C 4 quarter note beats in a measure
C means Common Time

The top number shows how many beats are in a measure.

The bottom number shows what sort of beats.
4 represents quarter notes.

2 quarter note beats in a measure $\frac{2}{4}$

1 2   1 2   1 2   1 2

Copy the above rhythm.

3 quarter note beats in a measure $\frac{3}{4}$

1 2 3   1 2 3   1 2 3   1 2 3

Copy the above rhythm.

4 quarter note beats in a measure $\frac{4}{4}$

1 2 3 4   1 2 3 4   1 2 3 4   1 2 3 4   1 2 3 4

Copy the above rhythm.

14

Match the measure with its time signature.

* *Count the beats in a measure and write in the time signatures.*

Write in the counts.

Count the beats in a measure and add the missing notes at the *.

Fill each measure with notes of different lengths to fit with time signature.

Accidentals

An accidental is a sharp, flat or natural that occurs in a piece of music.

♯	Sharp	*A sharp raises a note.*
♭	Flat	*A flat lowers a note.*
♮	Natural	*A natural restores a note to its original pitch.*

An accidental changes every following note in the measure that is on the same space or line.

An accidental is written in front of a note.

An accidental is written on the same line or in the same space as the note.

Write a sharp before each note.

example

Write a flat before each note.

example

Write a natural before each note.

example

Name the notes.

Name the notes.

Write the notes.

B♭   F♯   G♯   B♮   E♭   C♯   A♮

G♭   D♮   A♯   E♯   F♭   D♭   C♭

Write notes with accidentals but of different lengths so that every measure fits with the time signature.

When notes have the same letter name but are different pitches, another accidental is written.

Name the notes.

G♯   G♯

example

Write a tune in which every note is a flat.

Write a tune in which every note is a sharp.

Eighth Notes

♪ Eighth note ♪

𝄾 Eighth rest 𝄾

An eighth note is half of one quarter note.

The flag is always drawn on the right side of the stem.

Two eighth notes are usually beamed together to form a quarter note beat.

2 eighth notes = 1 quarter note

4 eighth notes = 1 half note

The first and/or last four eighth notes in a measure can be beamed together if they form half the measure, but never the middle four.

8 eighth notes = 1 whole note

Write groups of eighth notes and quarter notes.

Remember to check how many quarter note beats are in a measure.

Ledger Lines

Ledger lines extend the staff up and down. Notes are written in exactly the right position.

Ledger lines are small lines for notes written above or below the staff.

Ledger lines are like an invisible staff.

D C B A G

Name these notes.

G A B C D G A B C

Join the notes to the correct letter name.

A **B** **D** **G** **F** **C** **B** **A**

Write these notes using high and low ledger lines.

D A G B C A C G C B

✎ Check 2 How much do you remember?

Mix and Match Match the time signature to its description.

Four quarter notes in a measure   **2/4**

Three quarter notes in a measure   **4/4**

Two quarter notes in a measure   **3/4**

Quick Check Are the letters correct? Tick or cross the answers.

G F♭ C♯ F   G A A A A♭   A A B♭ D   G F♭ E♭ A♯

Quiz True or false? Circle the right answer.

1. Two eighth notes add up to one quarter note.   True   False

2. Four eighth notes add up to one half note.   True   False

3. A natural sign is not an accidental.   True   False

4. A time signature's top number tells us what sort of beat is in a measure.

                                                         True   False

5. A time signature's bottom number tells us what sort of beat is in a measure.

                                                         True   False

How many did you get right? ☐

Major Scales

All major scales have the same tune based on the steps between notes.

The steps that make up a scale are called whole steps and half steps.

Scales are a series of notes going up and down in steps.

All major scales have the same pattern of whole and half steps.

An octave is an interval of eight notes. From low C to high C is an octave.

C major scale (one octave) ascending

whole step whole step half step whole step whole step whole step half step

C major scale (one octave) descending

half step whole step whole step whole step half step whole step whole step

Draw a bracket above the half step intervals in these two scales.

G major scale (one octave) ascending (F#)

whole step whole step half step whole step whole step whole step half step

D major scale (one octave) ascending (F# and C#)

Write in the missing notes and name the scale.

C ....

Copy the scale exactly.

Key Signatures

Key signatures are sharps or flats at the start of each staff and show which scale is being used in the music.

A key signature of
1 sharp is F♯
2 sharps is F♯ C♯
3 sharps is F♯ C♯ G♯.

A key signature of
1 flat is B♭
2 flats is B♭ E♭
3 flats is B♭ E♭ A♭.

The key of C major has no sharps or flats.

The key of G major has one sharp, F♯.

The key of F major has one flat, B♭.

The key of D major has two sharps, F♯ and C♯.

The key of B♭ major has two flats, B♭ and E♭.

Join the key name to the key signature.

G major   C major   F major   D major   B♭ major

No sharps or flats   F♯ C♯   B♭ E♭   F♯   B♭

Write the key signatures.

G major   D major

In what key is this phrase? ....

In what key is this phrase? ....

Write the treble clef and the key signature for the scales that start on these notes.

Write the treble clef, the key signature and the scale of G major ascending.

Write the treble clef, the key signature and the scale of D major ascending.

Sometimes the key of a tune or phrase is shown by accidentals, perhaps because it has changed key.

Write the key of these phrases.

Write a phrase in G major that includes accidentals. Start and finish on G.

More Major Scales

Major scales with flats have the same tune as those with sharps.

Remember, All major scales have the same pattern of whole steps and half steps whether they use sharps or flats.

F major scale (one octave) ascending (B♭)

whole step whole step half step whole step whole step whole step half step

F major scale (one octave) descending (B♭)

Draw a bracket above the half step intervals.

B♭ major scale (one octave) ascending (B♭ E♭)

Draw a bracket above the half step intervals.

B♭ major scale (one octave) descending (B♭ E♭)

Draw a bracket above the half step intervals.

Write in the missing notes and name these scales.

Write a phrase in F major that includes accidentals. Start and finish on F.

Write in the missing notes and name these scales.

Write the scale of F major ascending.

Write the scale of B♭ major one octave ascending.

Write a phrase in B♭ major that includes accidentals. Start and finish on B♭.

Dotted Quarter Notes

♩ Dotted quarter note
𝄿 Dotted quarter rest

A dot after a note adds half its value to that note.

♩. = ♩ + ♪
1½ = 1 + ½

♩. = ♪ + ♪ + ♪
1½ = ½ + ½ + ½

$1\frac{1}{2}$

A dotted quarter note is often followed by an eighth note. Together they add up to 2 quarter notes.

Add up the notes and match them to the counts.

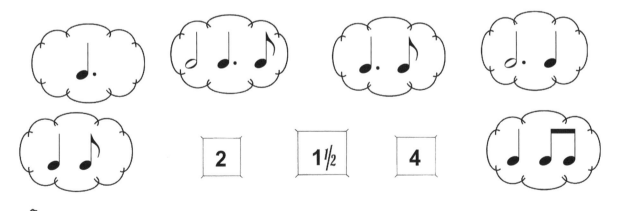

Write a dotted quarter note rhythm in each measure.

✎ Write the number of beats in the box.

○ = ☐ quarter notes

○· = ☐ half notes

𝅗𝅥 = ☐ eighth notes

♩ = ☐ eighth notes

○· = ☐ quarter notes

𝅗𝅥· = ☐ quarter notes

♩· = ☐ quarter notes

𝅗𝅥· = ☐ eighth notes

♩· = ☐ eighth notes

✎ Write in the missing quarter note counts.

1 2+ .... 3 4 1 + ... + 1 ....

✎ Copy the above tune exactly.

✎ Write a phrase that includes a dotted quarter note rhythm. Begin and end on G.

✎ Write a phrase that includes a dotted quarter note rhythm. Begin and end on C.

Add a dotted note to make each measure the correct length.

Match the note with the rest of the same length.

Write in the counts.

1 2

Write the scale of G major in dotted quarter notes and eighth notes.

Write the scale of F major in dotted quarter notes and eighth notes.

✎ **Check 3** How much do you remember?

Hurray! You are more than half way through the book. Good going!

Mix and Match Match the scale with its key signature.

C major scale   F#

G major scale   B♭

F major scale   No ♯ No ♭

Quick Check Are the key signatures correct? Tick or cross the answers.

 Cmajor

 Fmajor

 Gmajor

Quiz True or false? Circle the right answer.

1. A dot next to a note doubles the note in length.   True   False

2. Key signatures are written at the start of a line.   True   False

3. The scale of G major has B flat.   True   False

4. Whole steps and half steps are intervals between notes.

True   False

5. All major scales have different patterns of whole steps and half steps.

True   False

How many did you get right?

Degrees of the Scale

Degrees of the Scale
The first note of a scale is the keynote or 1st degree. The second note is the 2nd degree and the third is the 3rd degree. This contunues until the 8th degree or octave.

So the third degree in C major is the note E.

Degrees of the Scale

C major

1st — Keynote
2nd
3rd
4th
5th
6th
7th
8th — Octave

Write the degree of the scale in the key of C major.

example

3rd   5th   1st   8th

Write the degree of the scale in the key of F major. (F is the 1st degree)

example

8th   4th   6th   2nd

Write the degree of the scale in the key of G major. (G is the 1st degree)

example

2nd   3rd   8th   5th

Write a phrase in C major using only the 1st, 2nd, 3rd and 5th degrees of the scale.

Write a phrase in C major using only the 8th, 6th, 5th and 4th degrees of the scale.

Intervals

Match the interval with its description.

Minor Scales

Relatives
Each minor scale shares a key signature with a major scale. They are related.

The relative minor keynote is the sixth note of the major scale.

There are three kinds of minor scale. They are:
the natural minor scale,
the harmonic minor scale,
the melodic minor scale.
(In Book 2)

The natural minor scale has exactly the same notes as its relative major. But it starts on the 6th note of the major scale.

In C major, the sixth note of the scale is A. So A minor is the relative minor.

A natural minor scale (relative major is C major)

whole step half step whole step whole step half step whole step whole step

Draw a bracket above the half step intervals.

D natural minor scale (relative major is F major)

Draw a bracket above the half step intervals.

E natural minor scale (relative major is G major)

Write a phrase using only the notes of the A natural minor scale. Begin and end on A.

36

Write in the missing notes and name the scale.

Write in the A natural minor scale ascending and descending.

Write in the E natural minor scale ascending and descending.

Pair up the minor key with its key signature and relative major.

C major

F major

G major

D minor

E minor

A minor

F♯

No sharps or flats

B♭

Harmonic Minor Scales

The harmonic minor scale is the same as the natural minor but the 7th degree is raised by one half step.

In A natural minor scale the 7th note is G, and becomes G# in the harmonic minor.

Write a # by the 7th degree and complete the scale name.

.... harmonic minor scale

D harmonic .... scale

E .... minor scale

Write in the A harmonic minor scale ascending and descending.

Write in the D harmonic minor scale ascending and descending.

Arpeggios

Arpeggios are made from the 1st, 3rd, 5th and 8th degrees of the scale.

Major and minor arpeggios are made in the same way.

The interval between the 1st and 3rd notes in a minor scale is called a minor 3rd and is made up of three half steps.

C major scale

① ③ ⑤ ⑧

1 2 3 4 5 6 7 8

A natural minor scale

① ③ ⑤ ⑧

1 2 3 4 5 6 7 8

C major arpeggio

major third

A minor arpeggio

minor third

Colour in the notes that form the arpeggios in the scales below.

F major scale

G major scale

Remember to count from the lowest note of the scale.

Colour in the notes that form the arpeggios in the scales below.

C major scale

D natural minor scale

Write the arpeggio with its key signature. Use any note value.

F major

D minor

G major

E minor

Write a phrase using only the notes from C major arpeggio.

Write a phrase using only the notes from D minor arpeggio.

Write a phrase using only the notes from G major arpeggio.

✎ Check 4 How much do you remember?

Mix and Match Match the scale with its key signature.

A minor scale   F#

E minor scale   B♭

D minor scale   No # No ♭

Quick Check Are the arpeggios correct? Tick or cross them.

A minor arpeggio   *G major arpeggio*   *F major arpeggio*

Quiz True or false? Circle the right answer.

1. A natural minor scale has exactly the same notes as C major scale.

    True   False

2. An octopus is an interval of eight notes.   True   False

3. Each minor scale shares a key signature with a major scale.   True   False

4. Arpeggios are made from the 1st, 3rd, 5th and 7th notes of a scale.   True   False

5. D minor and F major share a key signature.   True   False

How many did you get right?

Musical Symbols

In music, symbols are used to show musical detail e.g. whether to play loud or quiet (dynamics) or how to bow, and many others. Here are a few of the most commonly used.

 gradually louder

gradually quieter

Bowing

V *Up-bow (bow travels from point to frog)*

⊓ *Down-bow (bow travels from frog to point)*

, *Bow lift (lift the bow and return it to its starting point)*

Slur -joined smoothly

Fermata - pause on the note

Phrase mark - showing one musical phrase

Accent - stressed, strongly

Staccato - short, detached

Tenuto - held and given pressure, broadly

Trill- alternate rapidly to the note above

Musical Terms

Italian words are often used in music to show tempo (speed), dynamics (louds and softs) and directions. Many of them are abbreviated. Here are some of the most commonly used.

accelerando / accel. - *gradually faster*

adagio - *slow*

allegretto - *fairly fast (but not as fast as allegro)*

allegro - *fast*

andante - *at a medium (walking) speed*

crescendo / cresc. - *gradually louder*

da capo / D.C. - *repeat from the beginning*

dal segno / D.S. - *repeat from the sign*

decrescendo / decresc. - *gradually quieter*

diminuendo / dim. - *gradually quieter*

dolce - *sweetly*

fine - *the end*

f **/ forte** - *loud*

ff **/ fortissimo** - *very loud*

grazioso - *graceful*

largo - *slow, stately*

legato - *smoothly*

mezzo - *moderately*

mf **/ mezzo forte** - *moderately loud*

mp **/ mezzo piano** - *moderately quiet*

moderato - *moderately*

p **/ piano** - *quiet*

pp **/ pianissimo** - *very quiet*

presto - *fast*

rallentando / rall. - *gradually slower*

ritenuto / rit. - *held back*

tempo - *speed, time (a tempo - in time)*

vivace - *lively, fast*

Bowing and Special Effects

arco - *play with the bow (often used after a pizzicato section)*

au talon - *play with the bow at the frog*

col legno - *'with the wood' – strike the string with the stick of the bow rather than the hair*

pizzicato - *plucked instead of bowed*

punta d'arco - *bow at the point of the bow*

sul ponticello - *play with the bow near the bridge*

Metronome Marking

♩ = **76** *76 quarter notes in a minute*

✎ *Rearrange these dynamic markings from quietest to loudest.*

p   *f*   *mf*   *ff*   *pp*   *mp*

....

✎ *Join the term, abbreviation and symbol to its description.*

rallentando   gradually quieter   gradually louder   crescendo

cresc.   rall.

accel.   accelerando

diminuendo   gradually slower   gradually faster   dim.

✎ *Write the symbol.*

Staccato   Accent   Down-bow   Fermata

✎ *Add symbols and dynamics to this phrase of music. Be as creative as you like!*

✎ *Write a phrase that changes tempo gradually.*

✎ *Write a phrase that changes dynamic gradually.*

Repeats and Directions

Repeat from the
beginning

Repeat the
section

D.S.	*Dal Segno*	Repeat from the sign
𝄋	*Segno*	Sign
D.S. al Coda		Repeat from the sign and then play the Coda
⊕	*Coda*	A coda is a phrase that ends a piece of music.
D.C.	*Da Capo*	Go back to the beginning
D.C. al Fine		Go back to the beginning and play to Fine

First-time Bars and Second-time Bars

When a composer wants a tune to be repeated but with a different ending the second time, he or she might use First-time Bars and Second-time Bars instead of writing out the tune in full.

First-time ending (play this the first time)

Second-time ending (on the repeat, play this ending instead)

Create a trail. Draw arrows to show where you go and explain the dynamic markings.

Dizzy Demon
from our Demon Studies book

Check 5 How much do you remember?

Mix and Match Match the term with its definition.

D.S.	moderately loud
D.C.	gradually faster
pp	gradually quieter
mf	gradually slower
Allegro	at a medium (walking) speed
Andante	gradually louder
diminuendo	repeat from the beginning
crescendo	very quiet
rallentando	repeat from the sign
accelerando	quick

Quick Check Are the symbols correct? Tick or cross them.

Staccato

Accent   Slur

Pause   Tenuto

Quiz True or false? Circle the right answer.

1. D.C. means go back to the sign. True False

2. Trills move from the written note to the note below. True False

3. **Fine** means 'the beginning'. True False

4. An accent is shown by a little arrow. True False

5. A staccato note is shown by a dot. True False

6. First and Second-time Bars are different endings. True False

7. D.S. means go back to the beginning. True False

How many did you get right?

Fantastic work! You've nearly finished. What a mover!

The Violin

How well do you know your violin?

✏ Draw arrows to the parts of the violin and bow.

Scroll

Tuning Pegs

Pegbox

Neck

Fingerboard

Front / Top

Upper bout

Winding / Wrapping

Eye

Ferrule

Frog / Heel

Tension screw

Bow hair

Stick

Headplate

Head

Tip or point

Bridge

Fine tuners

Tailpiece

Lower bout

F-holes

Strings

Chinrest

Violin Care

*After playing, loosen your bow, and dust the rosin off your violin with a soft cloth, checking under the strings and close to the bridge where rosin can easily build up.

*Remember to wipe the fingerboard and strings, and try not to play if you have sticky fingers!

*Avoid touching the bow hair because oil from your skin will stop the bow from playing well.

*Always pick up the bow by its frog, remembering to loosen the hair after each playing to let it rest and keep the bow from warping.

The Range of the Violin

The Violin Family

Today's Violins

Modern violin

Modern Baroque violin

Ultra-modern violin

Electric violins

The violin family also includes the viola, cello and double bass.

Ancestors of the Violin

Lira da braccio

Rebec

Medieval fiddle

Hardanger fiddle

Famous Violins

The 'Messiah' violin made by the Stradivari workshop in 1716 and now in the Ashmolean Museum, Oxford.

'Il Cannone Guarneri' made by the Guarneri workshop in 1743 was played by Paganini and is now in the town hall of Genoa, Italy.

'Le Marien' Stradivarius violin of 1714 was stolen in Manhatten, New York in 2002. It has never been found.

The String Family

Circle the instrument that is not a member of the string family.

Violin

Viola

Cello

Harp

Double Bass

Guitar

Piano

Interesting Violin Facts

The world record in cycling backwards playing a violin is 60.45 kilometres in 5 hours 8 seconds.

The worlds smallest violin is only 37 millimetres long and is small enough to fit in a box of matches.

The best quality bow hair comes from stallions from Mongolia, Siberia and Canada where the cold weather makes the hair stronger. It is usually black. White bow hair is usually bleached.

Famous people who played the violin include: Albert Einstein (physicist), Charlie Chaplin (actor), Thomas Jefferson (U.S. president), Marlene Dietrich (singer), Michael Angarano (actor), Chris Rankin (actor), Henri Rousseau (artist), Dolly Parton (singer), David Bowie (singer), Louis Farrakahn (activist), Paul Klee (artist), Jayne Mansfield (actor), and Henry Ford (industrialist).

Currently, the most expensive violin, is the Vieuxtemps Guarneri, made by Guarneri in 1741, which was sold for over £12 million in 2013. It had been played by Yehudi Menuhin among others. Its anonymous buyer has lent it to concert violinist, Anne Akiko Meyers.

Originally violin strings were made out of sheep gut, (but called catgut) now some strings have a nylon core wound in metal, others are steel wires wound with metal. The windings can be made of aluminium, silver, tungsten, chrome-steel or even gold.

Violins are usually made with a spruce top and a maple back, neck and sides, ebony fingerboard, and rosewood, ebony or boxwood pegs and tailpiece. More expensive violins have a hand-carved back and top and the wood is selected for its pattern and its potential for a great sound.

Purfling is the decorative inlay on the top and back of most violins. It is a sort of reinforcement, and can stop cracks and limit damage if a violin is bumped or knocked.

Rosin comes from sap that is tapped from conifer trees. The resin is heated and ingredients such as: essential oils, beeswax, gold, silver, tin or iron are added to a secret recipe. Violin rosin is designed to suit the violin's strings and is not as sticky as cello or double bass rosin.

Bows are often made from Brazilwood or Pernambuco. Both are woods and come from the same tree but Pernambuco is from the dense heartwood of the tree and produces a bow that can withstand greater tension.

The 'guage' of a string means 'thickness' and it affects the loudness and tone quality A thicker string will be louder and slower to respond. Strings are produced in three guages: light, medium and heavy.

Final Check

Wordsearch

```
C  D  H  Y  A  N  D  A  N  T  E  K  I  M  D
O  D  N  E  C  S  E  R  C  P  T  T  P  E  L
C  K  G  R  A  Z  I  O  S  O  E  G  C  O  T
A  O  F  S  E  V  Z  K  T  N  O  R  M  T  V
B  K  D  C  V  I  P  A  U  T  E  I  L  U  I
O  B  L  N  W  O  C  T  A  S  S  A  O  N  V
F  O  R  T  E  C  O  T  C  S  R  T  M  E  A
D  R  I  N  A  U  R  E  I  G  T  B  I  T  C
A  U  X  T  A  O  N  T  O  E  E  M  S  I  E
L  L  S  J  P  D  R  I  R  W  A  G  S  R  Y
E  S  L  E  O  O  B  G  M  R  K  M  I  P  A
G  C  B  E  F  T  E  P  C  I  E  P  N  I  R
A  L  A  B  G  L  T  A  P  Z  D  J  A  A  W
T  E  S  H  L  R  T  V  Z  T  V  N  I  N  E
O  F  S  A  C  O  O  O  T  S  E  R  P  O  L
```

 Can you find these words?

ALLEGRETTO	LEGATO
ALLEGRO	MEZZO
ANDANTE	PIANO
BASS	PIANISSIMO
CLEF	PRESTO
CRESCENDO	RITENUTO
DECRESCENDO	SLUR
DIMINUENDO	STACCATO
DOLCE	TENUTO
FORTE	VIVACE
FORTISSIMO	
GRAZIOSO	
LARGO	

Can you find these words?

BOW
BRIDGE
DOWNBOW
FERRULE
FHOLES
FINGERBOARD
FROG
GAUGE
GUARNERI
HARDANGER
LIRADABRACCIO
MAPLE
PEGS
PERNAMBUCO
PURFLING
REBEC
ROSIN
SCROLL
SHEEPGUT
STRADIVARIUS

```
            A  S  Q  Q              E  X  R  G
         E  L  D  Q  G  L        U  L  A  Y  O  P
         P  B  I  Z  S  D  Q  R     L  W  P  N  G  F  S  Y
         O  R  E  F  E  Q  N  Z  T  I  Q  K  W  A  Q  E  P  Z  I  Q
         Z  H  U  O  C  E  T  L  B  D  Q  L  H  H  M  B  K  K  X  H  N  Q
         L  S  C  R  O  L  L  H  A  R  D  A  N  G  E  R  L  B  S  Y  B  M  S  A
         I  C  Q  G  I  S  C  E  F  R  O  G  B  P  F  H  O  L  E  S  L  J  G  F
         D  L  Z  Z  K  P  T  N  X  X  L  I  R  A  D  A  B  R  A  C  C  I  O  N
         E  R  J  E  C  U  E  R  A  J  E  G  U  A  G  B  C  U  Z  H  Z  X  E  M
         J  G  D  I  E  H  S  R  A  M  B  D  O  W  N  B  O  W  K  W  C  L  K  X
         I  U  D  W  B  L  Y  Y  N  D  R  K  C  F  I  N  G  E  R  B  O  A  R  D
         R  X  I  E  M  K  Q  P  A  I  U  E  M  S  R  F  M  I  D  A  B  R
         J  E  S  R  O  Z  N  Y  I  M  V  R  Q  V  M  T  K  I  L  Z  L  Z
         O  N  H  B  L  A  J  S  S  B  A  G  E  L  U  R  R  E  F  H
         X  R  E  F  M  R  G  G  G  U  R  B  U  G  U  R  R  W
         B  A  E  H  E  S  D  N  U  C  I  I  E  R  T  R
         Z  U  P  Y  I  X  I  L  Q  O  U  B  C  V
         H  G  G  N  W  L  J  N  S  P  S  X
         H  X  U  Y  F  D  W  B  T  E
         B  V  T  R  O  D  B  A
         A  J  U  O  T  X
         F  P  C  H
         G  I
```

Wow!
Congratulations!
You've finished.
What a great
achievement.

The Violinist's Progress

Tick the box for each topic completed.

☐ Treble Clef

☐ Letter Names

☐ Note Values

☐ Stems

☐ Rests

☐ Check 1

☐ Time Signatures

☐ Accidentals

☐ Eighth Notes

☐ Ledger Lines

☐ Check 2

☐ Major Scales

☐ Key Signatures

☐ More Major Scales

☐ Dotted Quarter Notes

☐ Check 3

☐ Degrees of the Scale

☐ Intervals

☐ Minor Scales

☐ Arpeggios

☐ Check 4

☐ Musical Symbols

☐ Musical Terms

☐ Repeats and Directions

☐ Check 5

☐ The Violin

☐ The Violin Family

☐ The String Family

☐ Interesting Violin Facts

☐ Final Check

Congratulations

to

....

for completing

The Vibrant Violin Music Theory Book 1!

If you have enjoyed **The Vibrant Violin Music Theory Book 1** why not try the other books in the **Vibrant Violin** series!

For more info, please visit: **WildMusicPublications.com**

All of our books are available to download, or you can order from Amazon.

Introducing some of our favourites:

Violin Practice Notebook

50+ Greatest Classics

Christmas Carols

Trick or Treat – A Halloween Suite

Intermediate Classic Duets

Fish 'n' Ships

Easy Duets from Around the World

Christmas Duets

Violin Music Theory Book 2

Christmas Duets for Violin and Viola

Easy Traditional Duets for Flute and Violin

Intermediate Classic Duets for Descant Recorder and Violin

More Christmas Duets for Violin and Cello

Very Easy Christmas Duets for Teacher and Pupil

Champagne and Chocolate

Moonlight and Roses

Christmas Crackers

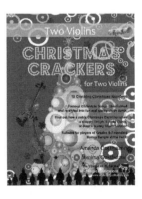

Easy Tunes from Around the World

Christmas Bonanza

Easy Classic Duets

Easy Traditional Duets

Manufactured by Amazon.ca
Bolton, ON